MW00955479

WILD HORSES!
SCIENTIFIC FACTS FOR KIDS
WHO LOVE HORSES
CHILDREN'S BIOLOGICAL SCIENCE OF HORSES BOOKS

BOBO'S
LITTLE BRIANIAC BOOKS

educational & informative books for children
(PRE-K / K-12)

What do you know
about wild horses?
Are they dangerous?

Long ago, all horses were wild animals. All horses are grazers: they eat grass and other plants.

Horses have long been associated with humans because of their beauty and power. Only two subspecies of the original wild horse survive. They are the Przewalski's horse and the domesticated horse.

It is believed that the Przewalski's horse is the last true wild horse. Its ancestors were never domesticated.

In the 1500s, Spanish explorers brought horses to America. It was believed that some of those horses escaped to live in the wild.

Wild horses
live in western
states like Idaho
and Colorado.
Some are also
on islands off
the east coast.
Pockets of
wild horses
also roam in
Europe, Australia
and Asia.

Today, in some parts of America, the wild horses known as mustangs are still found roaming. They are the descendants of the horses brought by the European explorers and settlers.

Wild horses have stronger legs than domestic horses. With their hard hooves, they run well in different types of ground conditions.

Wild horses look mangy and dirty because they love rolling in the dust and nobody brushes or combs them.

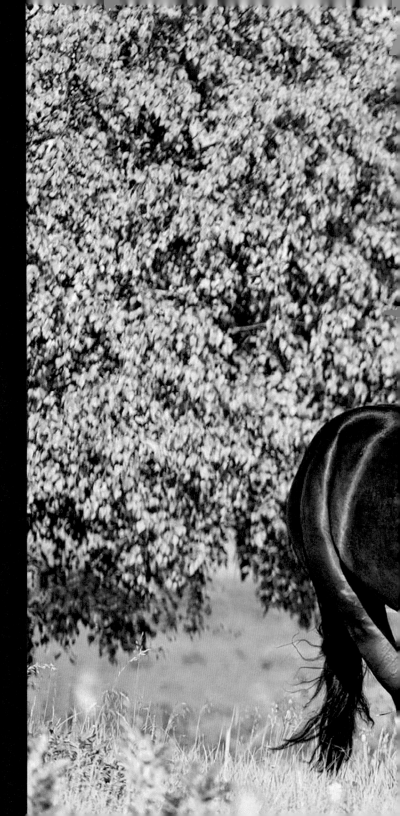

They come in different colors, such as black, grey and white. But most of the wild horses are reddish brown or roan in color.

Mares, or female horses, can weigh up to 317 kilograms and stallions, or male horses,can weigh up to 450 kilograms.

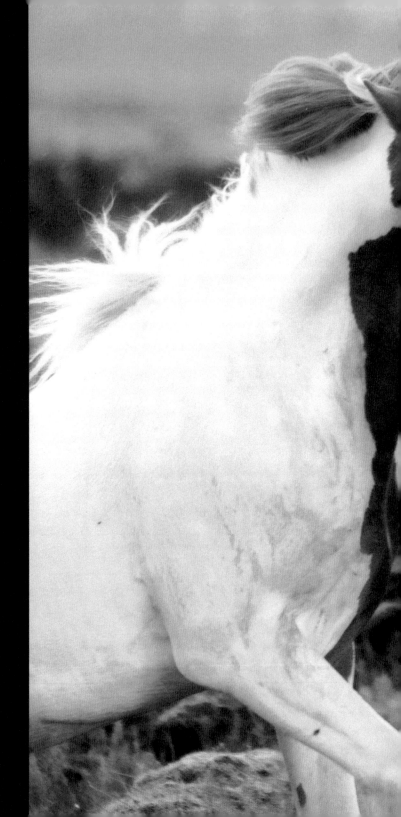

Horses love
to eat grass,
although they
also graze on
leaves, twigs
and tree bark.

A new-born baby horse is called a foal. When it turns two years old, the female foal is called a filly and the male foal is called a colt. After six years, the filly is called a mare and the colt becomes a stallion.

Wild horses
are sociable.
They usually
stay together
in groups called
herds. This
is for their
protection. The
herd is headed
by one adult
male followed by
harem of mares
and their young.

Once a colt becomes a stallion it either challenges the herd leader or just leaves the group to try to make its own herd. The stallion has to protect the herd from predators.

Unfortunately, wild horses are decreasing in number. But there are organizations that try to maintain wild horse population.

Wild horses in
Australia are
called brumbies.

When mares get pregnant it lasts for 335-340 days. The mare will then give birth to a single foal or, rarely, twins. The foals, shortly after birth, are capable of standing and running.

Horses are our long-time friends. They are with us wherever we may like to take them. Whether in the wild or domesticated, horses are worthy of human care.

Made in the USA
Las Vegas, NV
01 July 2023

74101999R00026